TEACHER'S GUIDE

&

STUDENT QUIZZES

by

Daniel Schwabauer

ONE YEAR
ADVENTURE
NOVEL

Teacher's Guide

&

Student Quizzes

The One Year Adventure Novel
Teacher's Guide and Student Quizzes
by Daniel Schwabauer

Clear Water Press
PO Box 62
Olathe, KS 66051
www.clearwaterpress.com

Printed in the USA

This book is intended for the education of its readers. Any
similarities between characters mentioned herein and
persons living or dead is purely coincidental. Any slights of
people, places or organizations are unintentional.

Cover design by CDS Creative Design.

ISBN 978-0-9742972-7-9

CONTENTS

"Every writer I know has trouble writing."

~Joseph Heller

Introduction

I hope you aren't intimidated by the presence of a Teacher's Guide with this curriculum. I know many parent educators have little time to prepare lessons. *The One Year Adventure Novel* is designed to be easy to use and requires very little preparation. You don't have to read this book before your student begins.

The purpose of this book is twofold. First, it's meant to assist you in helping your student become a better writer. Second, it contains a simple method for evaluating and grading your student's work, which can be hard to do objectively without a system.

I suggest that you read the first two chapters of this Teacher's Guide by the end of the first month, and watch the DVD lesson called *For Parents and Teachers*. The *Frequently Made Mistakes* video on the resource disk would also be helpful to watch.

The One Year Adventure Novel can be used in place of one year of high school English, or as a supplement to your regular English curriculum.

1

About the Curriculum

How to use this curriculum

The One Year Adventure Novel is designed to take high school students through the process of writing a structured adventure novel over the course of one school year. The complete curriculum includes a textbook (*The Compass*), a workbook (*The Map*), this *Teacher's Guide*, a set of DVD discs containing video lessons of all 78 lessons, and Anthony Hope's classic adventure tale, *The Prisoner of Zenda*. Bonus materials include over a dozen classic adventure novels in electronic format (designed to be printed on 8.5 x 11 paper from your home computer), various printouts and weekly quizzes, video FAQs and a number of additional features on the Resource Disk.

It is designed to be teacher-friendly. You do not need to know how to write a novel to take your student through this class. All of the instruction is done through video disc and reading (and, of course, writing, which is a very instructive exercise.)

The curriculum should take about one school year, September through May, to complete. Students may complete the course on either a three-lesson-per-week or a five-lesson-per-week schedule.

Either way, using the curriculum is easy. Before you begin, watch the introductory video, *How to Use this Curriculum* on DVD. If possible, try to read the first two chapters of this Teacher's Guide in the first few weeks of the course.

Each day, your student will begin by watching the video lesson for that day. Most of the lessons are 10 or 15 minutes long. Some run longer, and a few are a bit shorter.

After watching the video lesson, your student should read the corresponding lesson in *The Compass* and read any assigned reading selections for the day. Finally, your student will answer the questions in *The Map* (first semester) or write their rough draft based on the story outline they've created (second semester).

Each week you should administer the weekly quiz. This can done verbally using the quiz questions included in a later chapter of this book, or, even easier, by computer. Simply insert the Resource Disk into your home computer and launch the OYAN Desktop. From the desktop, access the quiz program, and select the week. The computer will lead your student through that week's quiz and assign a grade.

Additional helpful resources are available on the Resources disk and online at www.oneyearnovel.com.

What makes OYAN different?

This curriculum is focuses on storytelling and creativity, rather than on grammar and mechanics. However, this does not mean that the curriculum is unstructured. Teachers sometimes wrongly assume that creativity will result from removing boundaries, from "thinking outside the box."

I'm a huge fan of creative thinking. I love outside-the-box thinkers. But creativity doesn't come from having no structure. The only thing that comes from having no structure is confusion.

For example, have you ever given your student a creative writing assignment with no (or few) rules? "Here, Johnny. I'm giving you a blank sheet of paper. I want you to write a story about *anything you want!*"

The results of such assignments are usually much less than satisfactory. You may read such an assignment and marvel at the results because they are not what you expected. "Wow!" you say. "What an imagination!"

Indeed. But did the story hold together as a story? Was it really *good*? Are there any other factors in the story worthy of admiration? Is it basically one unexpected thing after another? Or is it a carbon copy of a movie you watched last week with ever-so-slightly changed characters?

Truth is, there is nothing more intimidating to any writer than a blank sheet of paper. Even lined paper is better than blank, because the lines give definition and a goal to shoot for. (*If I just write twenty five lines worth of stuff, I'm done.*)

Remember this: the freedom to choose anything does not inspire creativity. It inspires panic.

Boundaries inspire creativity. Limitations inspire creativity. Guidelines inspire creativity.

I'm not talking about rigidity. Boundaries without freedom are just as damaging to the imagination as having no boundaries at all. I'm talking about adding guidance to freedom. I'm talking about setting up some guardrails and saying, "Let's go West." Rather than telling Johnny to write about anything, tell him to write a story about a shipwreck, or a voyage to Mars, or a prince who loses his crown. A voyage to Mars is guidance. It's a goal. How Johnny gets to Mars is freedom. Boundaries and limitations are fuel for the fire of the imagination. The freedom to choose within those limitations is air. A good fire needs both.

This is the approach I've adopted in the *One Year Adventure Novel*. Boundaries combined with freedom.

I've also taken a number of liberties in my approach to traditional writing concepts. Most English courses rightly stress the five elements of literature in discussing the novels of Twain, Kipling or Lewis: characterization, plot, setting, theme and style. These are important concepts to understand when analyzing a work of literature. However, they are most unhelpful when writing a rough draft. They are concepts of analysis, not creativity. I doubt anyone—including Twain, Kipling or Lewis—ever wrote a readable novel because they focused their imagination on a literary concept like characterization. Readable story characters come from focusing on interesting people, not abstract ideas.

I believe the most effective approach to teaching students how to write fiction is to begin by teaching concrete storytelling techniques which can later be used to shape the story in one's imagination into words on paper.

Therefore, our goal this year is, 1) to learn what makes a story a story, and 2) to write a compelling adventure novel over the course of the school year.

What to expect from your student

You know your student better than anyone. Your expectations should match his or her abilities. Students should be challenged but not frustrated.

Expect more from a senior than a freshman: not just more words, but more depth of thought, more complexity in characterization.

Remember, the goal of the curriculum is two-fold. The primary objective is to teach storytelling techniques that will enrich a student's writing and help him or her understand the impact stories have on real life. The secondary objective is to write a compelling novel.

Regarding the first: understanding story *matters*. It may matter to the life destiny of a teen more today than it ever has. Why? Every culture is shaped by its storytellers. In Africa, many tribes regard the village storyteller as the lawgiver and chief, the bearer of wisdom. In America, storytellers are seen differently, but their impact may be even greater. Consider the impact of the entertainment industry on the behavior of teens. It's no secret that popular culture has had a corrosive effect on the moral fiber of our country. It's the storytellers who steer popular culture.

Who are America's storytellers? In publishing, one might think of Stephen King, Tom Clancy, or J.K. Rowling. In the film industry, George Lucas and Stephen Spielberg come to mind. In truth, both Hollywood and New York are filled with production companies and publishers that rely on a small army of writes, actors, composers, directors, and editors to deliver the entertainment Americans crave.

But these are not our only storytellers. They may not even be our primary storytellers. Newspaper editors and journalists, television newscasters, politicians, marketing executives and ad writers, scientists, rap singers, talk radio hosts, and even university professors make their living telling stories. Some of these stories are based in truth. Some are outright lies. Most are a mixture of fact and fiction.

By learning how all storytellers manipulate an audience through emotion, young writers learn a valuable life lesson and gain understanding that will help them see the techniques that will be used against them—and occasionally for them—as they live life.

Regarding the secondary objective—writing a compelling adventure novel over one school year: the general guidelines below will give you an idea of what you might expect from your students based on their age. Keep in mind that these are only guidelines. Children mature differently; what may be appropriate for one sophomore may be too difficult for another, and too easy for someone else. Word count is not as important as understanding and incorporating the story techniques we discuss in the lessons.

Freshman (9th grade)   1,250 words per chapter
15,000 words (finished novel)

Sophomore (10th grade)   1,500 words per chapter
18,000 words (finished novel)

Junior (11th grade)   1,750 words per chapter
21,000 words (finished novel)

Senior (12th grade)   2,000 words per chapter
24,000 words (finished novel)

Formatted correctly (see the example in lesson 77 of *The Compass*), one page of manuscript text will equal about 250 words. So a Freshman should be able to write five pages per week during the second semester. Some will write considerably longer novels. Others may struggle to create five or six pages of rough draft material every week of the second semester. Some will naturally have a sparse style, and others will be naturally wordy.

And of course, every chapter will not be the same length. The point is to write a workable rough draft, not meet a word quota.

As long as your student is meeting your expectations— what you know they can do—they 're on the right track.

2

Guidance & Evaluation

How to help your student improve

Young writers need help. It isn't enough to be a good reader, or have a way with words, or love to write. It isn't enough to be talented. In order to improve, young writers need feedback from someone who cares. That means you.

Unfortunately, this may mean wading through many pages of less-than-perfect prose. Just as beginning musicians need the freedom to learn piano or violin by playing badly, young writers need the freedom to write badly so they can learn to write well.

One big difference between fiction and music is that wrong notes are obvious even to the untrained ear. A song badly played on the violin will be unpleasant even to the one playing it. But in writing, an author may not know that her story isn't working. Or she may know it doesn't work, but she doesn't understand why. She can't identify the sour notes from the sweet.

This is where you come in. Good instruction in proven storytelling techniques is not enough. Your student needs your help to figure out what works and what doesn't. Your student needs your thoughtful evaluation.

You don't have to be a writer to provide useful feedback. All you really need is a few simple pointers and a sincere desire to help your student improve.

First, don't think in terms of grading. Grading isn't the most important thing you can do for your student. When you read a paragraph, a page, or a chapter, take off your teacher hat and put on that of a reader. Don't focus on spelling or grammar. Try to read only for the sake of the story—for enjoyment.

In this curriculum I stress the importance of the imagination in the creative process. I do not teach students to ignore grammar and spelling, but I do teach them not to worry about grammar and spelling while they're creating. Spelling and comma splice errors will of course need to be fixed eventually, but not while writing a rough draft of a novel. These corrections are part of polishing, and involve analytical activity in the brain that can hinder creativity.

Because I tell students not to shut down their imagination in order to check the spelling of a word, I must also ask parents not to nit-pick at mechanical issues early in the creative process.

All stories are about creating emotion. Emotion is created through sensory images—movies, if you will—that are generated in the imagination. Stories that don't create emotion fail because they are boring. Boredom, after all, is simply the lack of emotion.

Your student is trying to create emotion in you, the reader, by conjuring images in your imagination. This process is difficult to master even when it is fully understood. To the student who doesn't yet fully understand it, the process can be frustratingly difficult.

This is where your help is so valuable. Few people really want to sit down and read a novel by a young writer. Novels take time to read, and first novels, because they are often bad, seem to take a *long* time. Who wants to spend several hours reading something dull—something that doesn't create emotion, doesn't involve compelling situations and characters, doesn't stand on its own internal logic?

The person who cares about the young writer enough to plow through a first novel will often love her too much to be brutally honest. No one will tell her, "It's boring." To do so would be cruel. Instead, your student is much more likely to hear, "It was good. I liked it."

She doesn't need to hear "It's boring," even if it is. This could damage her self-confidence so much that she gives up writing altogether. Neither does she need to hear, "It was good. I liked it." She knows her novel isn't perfect. She may know that it isn't really good—yet. And that makes well-intentioned, generic praise confusing. It was good? Really? What was good about it?

The young writer doesn't know what works and what doesn't, even in her own novel. Vague praise tends to reinforce the idea that her novel is either entirely good or entirely bad, when neither is the case.

In short, she needs specific feedback, not generalities. She needs someone to give her encouragement and honest evaluation.

Here's how you do it.

First, apply anything you already know about writing—either from personal experience or by listening to the lessons on DVD—to your student's prose. It's always easier to catch mistakes in someone else's work than it is in your own. If you have time to participate in the curriculum with your student you will be better equipped to understand why certain things do or do not work.

Second—and most important—be specific in your feedback on a page-by-page basis. This is the essence of being a good feedback reader. Your job is to tell your student exactly how each page made you feel and think. If you know why it made you feel something, great; tell your student that too. But if not, you're still performing an invaluable task. In effect, you're holding up a mirror to your student's manuscript so she can see it for what it really is. You're acting as her ears so she can hear the story music she's trying to play. You're allowing her to begin to differentiate between the sour notes and the sweet.

You need not be a writer to give honest and helpful feedback. Just read carefully and make notes on every page. Then sit down with your student and tell her how her work affected you. Always start with the positives, with what worked. Then move on to any weaknesses.

Here's an example of what honest feedback looks like:

"Rachel, I've finished your first chapter, and I am very pleased."

"Really?"

"Yes. Your characters are believable and their situation is very intriguing. And I liked the idea of setting the first chapter in the castle. I wouldn't have thought of that."

"I wanted to make it interesting."

"It is interesting. I especially liked the section on page five where your hero realizes she's been betrayed. The dialog in the middle of the page made me so angry for her."

"Good!"

"I also enjoyed the very end of the chapter when she's trapped in the tower with no way out. It made me want to keep reading."

"I wasn't sure how to spell moat."

"That's okay, you can look it up later. I do think you might improve the first page by cutting out the first paragraph."

"Really?"

"For some reason the first paragraph wasn't nearly as interesting as the rest of the story. And after I read the whole chapter it occurred to me that you don't really need to tell us when this is happening. Your readers will understand by the flavor of the book that it's happening during medieval times."

"Okay."

"Also, I got kind of bogged down on pages three and four. I'm not sure why, but those pages seemed less interesting than the rest of the chapter. Maybe you could shorten them or find something else for your hero to be doing instead of combing her hair."

"She *is* a princess."

"Indeed."

"But...I guess hair-combing isn't all that interesting?"

"Well, maybe you could make it interesting."

"How?"

"I don't know. What if something else was going on while she was combing her hair?"

"You mean like a fire?"

"Or just a conversation with someone. Instead of just thinking about things, maybe she could discuss what's on her mind with one of the castle servants."

"Oh, I know! What if she has a fight with her wicked stepmother!?"

"A fight?"

"You know...a *conflict.*"

"Such as?"

"What if her wicked stepmother is the one combing her hair, only each stroke is so hard that it hurts?"

"Wicked stepmother sounds mean."

"Of course she is. I'm writing an adventure novel. Anyway, that's a *great* idea. Thanks!"

"One more thing."

"Shoot."

"I don't think the guard at the gate would have let her through."

"He might have."

"True, but that isn't the point. When I was reading, it didn't seem believable to me. I didn't think the guard would do that without some reason."

"So, I should have her bribe the guard?"

"I just think there should be more of a trust or friendship between the guard and your hero. Otherwise I think he would have refused to let her through and he may have even told her father."

"But he's a new guard. How can they trust each other?"

"You'll think of something."

It isn't your role to find answers to the problems you find in your student's story. If you have suggestions, voice them. If not, it is enough to explain how the story made you feel, where it works and where it doesn't.

Frequently Made Mistakes

Beginning writers tend to make the same common mistakes. We discuss these mistakes repeatedly in the video lessons and in the textbook. However, some mistakes are very difficult to overcome because they're hard to see. Students can make any—or all—of these mistakes and not realize it. Again, your insight is vital to your student's perception of what she's written.

Read through the following descriptions and explanations of the ten most common mistakes young writers make when writing a first novel. Then watch the short video lesson, *Frequently Made Mistakes* with your student. (It's on the Resource Disk.) The video covers the same material, but the repetition should help you be more confident in spotting problems when you read. Catching even one or two of these mistakes in your student's manuscript will be extremely helpful.

1. The Hero doesn't act or decide. He isn't the motivating force behind the story events. The story happens to the Hero instead of the Hero happening to the story.

It's hard for readers to identify with the hero if he doesn't act heroic, and a huge part of acting heroic means taking action. The hero who is blown along by the winds of an unkind fate will seem weak at best, and pathetic at worst.

This doesn't mean the hero should succeed at everything he does. On the contrary, he should fail in every chapter. But he can only fail if he tries. If the story always pushes the hero around and he never pushes back, we won't like him as a hero.

To put it another way, the hero must be the reason stuff happens in the story. If the hero escapes from the villain's dungeon, it must be because he conks the guard over the head, or tunnels through rock with his bare hands, or swan dives into shark infested waters. It mustn't be because some stranger rescues him, or because the guard accidentally leaves his door open.

2. Point-of-View shifts. Showing things your Hero can't know or see.

POV shifts can be hard to spot even for experienced writers. Look for any information that seems to come from beyond the hero's perspective. POV shifts often involve telling instead of showing (see mistake #4), which means you may be able to spot them because they are conceptual in nature rather than sensual. That is, they give the reader an idea, not an image.

When in doubt, the simplest way to identify a POV shift is to ask yourself, *might the hero know this?* If not, it needs to be changed.

3. No conflict in a scene - especially in opening chapters.
Scenes that are neither disasters nor dilemmas, but
just one thing happening after another.

Lack of conflict will kill any story. And conflict isn't necessarily present simply because something is happening. Unfortunately, most beginning writers subconsciously tend to avoid conflict. They like their hero and don't want to see him hurt. They don't want him to suffer. They don't want the stress of conflict among their characters any more than they want the stress of conflict in real life. Writing is hard enough; must we add conflict to it as well?

Stories without conflict are boring. If your student grows bored with writing her adventure novel, chances are she doesn't have a compelling conflict to write about.

She may deny this. She may *think* she has a compelling conflict. ("But my book has pirates in it! Sea monsters and battles and kidnapping and poison and torture! What do you *mean* it doesn't have conflict?") Conflict means a clash of wills. As described in lessons 22 through 24, it comes in several forms, the most basic of which are disasters and dilemmas.

Your student might write scenes that avoid any real conflict by substituting defiant dialog or pointless chases for logical action that results in a disaster (an external conflict) or a dilemma (an internal conflict). Just because a scene has a sea-monster in it doesn't mean it has any real conflict. Does the hero fight the sea-monster? If so, does something bad happen as a result? Or, does he face a terrible choice between two negative alternatives?

If something bad doesn't as a result happen of the clash between sea-monster and hero, or if the hero isn't faced with a terrible decision that itself leads to something bad happening, your student's chapter or scene has no real conflict.

If necessary, read lesson 22 with your student and ask her to write down the levels of momentary conflict as they unfold in her chapter. She can do this in pairs of very short sentences that describe what the hero does to get something, and what happens to stop him. Put together, these momentary conflicts should add up to a disaster or a dilemma.

If your student can't identify a clear progression of increasingly desperate and consequential momentary conflicts that end in a dilemma or a disaster, the section needs to be rewritten. Once she's created interesting momentary conflicts, she'll find her chapter is much more fun to write.

4. Telling instead of showing. Passive voice sentences instead of sensory sentences. "Was" sentences.

The goal of every story is to create emotion. Novels do this by creating movies in the reader's imagination; images, sounds, smells, feelings, and even thoughts can be part of this internal movie.

Creating a movie in the reader's mind is much more difficult than simply telling a story. It requires precise and vivid details, which are harder to dream up than simple concepts. It's easy for me to tell you that my hero was in the desert and he was very hot. But this doesn't create a movie in your mind. It merely communicates information, and information rarely impacts one's emotions. *Telling* is a sign the writer hasn't clearly imagined her story for herself.

"It was hot" is conceptual. To make it sensual—that is, to change it from *telling* into *showing*—I must describe details that will create a movie in your mind. I must show you how hot the hero was, as in: "Sweat poured down his face. His feet blistered in his heavy leather boots, and his lips cracked and bled. His tongue was a lump of coal behind his teeth."

This is showing. Look for precise, unexpected sensory details that create images and sounds in your mind as you read. If you read any page and find yourself not imagining a

19

story clearly, or if the details don't seem real to you, your student is probably telling her story instead of showing it.

*5. Use of unnecessary or dull adjectives and any
    adverbs.*

Adjectives and adverbs are modifiers. They make something imprecise more specific. Adjectives make a car *red* or *fast* or *clean*. Adverbs tell us how someone did something. He walked *quickly*. The child smiled *happily*. Adjectives usually modify nouns, and adverbs modify verbs.

It isn't possible to remove all adjectives from a novel, but one can certainly try. Most students tend to use unnecessary adjectives. They modify nouns that don't need modification, or they tell us something that should be obvious from the noun itself. For example, "the *huge* elephant." Aren't elephants usually huge? If the word *elephant* weren't modified by the word *huge*, would we presume the beast was small? Of course not. The time to use an adjective is when the modification isn't obvious. "The tiny purple elephant" uses two very necessary adjectives to modify an elephant in ways we couldn't predict.

Similarly, adverbs always point to a weak verb. Most beginning writers rely on adverbs when they should be choosing vivid verbs that don't need modification. Encourage your student to remove every adverb and change their verbs to the most precise and vivid action words they can imagine (except when using dialog tags). Instead of "walking quietly" down a hallway, the hero might *tiptoe*, or *stalk*, or even *steal*. The adverb *quietly* points to *walked*, which is a relatively dull verb. The sentence would be improved by making the verb stronger and more vivid.

*6. Funky verbs used as dialog tags. Students having
    been taught to avoid "said."*

Dialog tags are those identifiers one finds in dialog, usually at the end of a sentence, that tell us who says what.
   "How's it going?" Jim asked.

"Fine," Marty replied.

Asked and *replied* here are examples of dialog tags. The most common tag in literature—especially modern literature —is *said*. *Said* is used so often it is essentially invisible. Because it is common, it is tempting to think that it is ineffective.

In fact, writing teachers sometimes encourage their students to replace "boring" dialog tags like *said, asked, replied, shouted* and *whispered* with more interesting verbs. As a result, I see many first novels with characters who never *say* anything. Instead, they *retort.* They *expostulate.* They *explode.* They *condescend.*

This is an unfortunate habit that must be broken. Please do not encourage your student to use unusual verbs as dialog tags.

Keep in mind what a dialog tag is for. It's there to identify who says what. It may also tell us *how* something is said (as in, *whispered, shouted,* etc.) It isn't there to give us any other information, or to supply action. This is why unusual verbs are problematic. They call attention to themselves and distract the reader from what was said.

"How's it going?" Jim expostulated.

"Fine," Marty retorted.

Said can be used as a dialog tag almost endlessly without distracting the reader. Better yet, encourage your student to leave off dialog tags altogether whenever possible. As a general rule of thumb, limit dialog tags to places where they're needed for the sake of clarity. Much of the time untagged dialog can stand on its own. For example, did you notice that I used no dialog tags at all in the example of honest feedback on pages 14-16?

7. Overusing an "ing" verb at the beginning of sentences to vary sentence structure.

This isn't something your student should avoid completely. Just make sure there isn't a participial phrase at the beginning of every other sentence.

The guiding principle is, if it sounds funny to you, it will sound funny to everyone else.

21

*8. Dialog that doesn't demonstrate conflict or advance
   the plot. Chit-chat that doesn't reveal who a
   character is. People talking about things for the sole
   purpose of giving information to the reader.*

Good, believable dialog is difficult to write. Ideally, the reader should feel as though she's eavesdropping on a real conversation, but with the boring parts (such as stuttering and "um" and conversational bunny-trails) left out.

Good dialog moves the plot forward and reveals something about the characters who are speaking.

It may help your student to hear her dialog read aloud. This is a simple way of identifying what works and what doesn't. Something that looks natural on the page doesn't always sound natural to the ear.

*9. Vague, obvious and boring details instead of precise,
   unexpected details. (Templates and cliches, i.e.
   fantasy market scenes with fishmongers "hawking
   their wares.")*

First novels are typically filled with descriptions that fail to inspire the imagination. Why? It's almost always because the writer has not taken the time to really imagine a scene for herself. Therefore, when she tries to put the scene into words, she relies on concepts. She describes an office building as ordinary, or a day as hot, or a man as good-looking.

These are easy ways of communicating an idea. They are the language of speech, and as such force of habit allows them into one's written work. But concepts do not create images and sounds in a reader's mind. Precise, unexpected details do.

This mistake is not the same as #4, because it applies even to scenes in which the author has provided details. But even if a scene is written with details—even if the writer is showing instead of telling—the details themselves may not be vivid or unexpected enough to hold the reader's interest. When writing a rough draft, it's easy for your student to describe things she hasn't imagined for herself. It's easy to

22

glom onto some bit of description she read in a book last week, *and not even know she's doing it.*

As you read, ask yourself what your imagination is doing. Is a setting vivid? Is the action of a page clear and compelling?

If you don't clearly see a movie in your mind as you read, your student is not giving you precise and unexpected details. She's asking you to imagine a story she hasn't really imagined clearly in her own mind.

10. Weasel words. Words and phrases to be avoided, such as "tried" (I tried to stay near the door), or "somewhat" (he was somewhat large) or "I don't know how it happened, but..."

Check the resource disk for a complete list of words to avoid. Many are on the list for reasons specific to themselves. Several are merely words of equivocation, which should be avoided.

Weasel words, like passive voice and adverbs, are hard to spot at first in one's own work. Once they are pointed out a few times, the beginning writer will begin to see them for herself. Eventually she'll stop using them altogether.

For now, you're her best chance of identifying the weasel words in her novel. Take a few minutes to look through the major ones below. When you spot one in your student's manuscript, circle it.

was	had	try	somewhat	somehow
rather	just	probably	that	realized
really	very	seemed	started	began
finally	suddenly			

3

How to Grade

How do you grade a novel—especially a first novel written by a high school student? Do you grade based on characterization? Plot? Spelling? Are there any concrete standards by which you can evaluate a student's work? Or do you grade based merely on effort?

It's obvious that grading is a difficult and imprecise aspect of teaching fiction. Because it is imprecise, you may be tempted—consciously or unconsciously—to use the more easily assessed elements of grammar and spelling to grade your student's work. *Cat* is spelled with a C, not a K. Because there's only one right way to spell *cat*, it's easy to point out where the student is wrong and how the problem can be fixed. It's also more fair. The fact that one can open a dictionary and point to the "accepted" spelling of *cat* lends an air of justice to the grading process.

The teacher of fiction has no universal dictionary of accepted storytelling standards by which to evaluate a student's work. Traditionally, this means she must either assign grades based on specific concepts addressed in class ("this week we're talking about verbs"), or based on a vague feeling about the quality of the student's work. Grading based on word count hardly seems fair, since anyone can churn out mere words in order to meet a word count; and words do not a story make.

The *One Year Adventure Novel* uses a mixed grading system. First semester grades are based on lesson scores (your student's answers to the questions in *The Map*) and weekly quiz scores. Second semester grades are based on chapter scores (your student's novel) and weekly quiz scores. Final grades are based on a combination of all three: lesson, chapter and quiz scores.

24

Lesson scores

Each day during the first semester your student will answer questions about his or her story in *The Map*. In the lower right hand corner of every lesson you'll find a scoring box. Scoring for each lesson is based on three simple rubrics that will help you evaluate your student's answers. For each rubric, assign a number between 1 and 10. High numbers are better than low numbers.

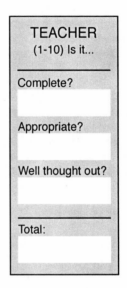

Complete: Did your student answer all the questions? Are the answers themselves complete?

Appropriate: Are the answers appropriate and relevant? Do they address the specific question asked?

Well thought out: Do the answers show a commitment to making the story as a whole work better? Are the answers consistent with the answers given in previous lessons?

After assigning a number for each rubric, enter the total of all three in the lowest box.

Weekly Quizzes

Each of the 26 weekly quizzes is worth 30 points, for a total of 780 points, or 24% of the final grade.

Quizzes can be given two ways. The easiest way is by computer. Simply insert the Resource Disk and double click the appropriate quiz. The quiz program will launch automatically. After your student answers the last question, the computer will provide a percentage grade. Divide the percentage grade by 3.33 and round to the nearest number.

This is the point grade for that quiz. Suppose, for example, that your student earned a 93% on one quiz:

$$93 \div 3.33 = 27.9 \text{ (round up to 28)}$$

For each quiz, enter the number of points earned on the appropriate scoring sheet in chapter five.

Quizzes may also be given verbally. A copy of every quiz is provided for this purpose in chapter four. To determine quiz grades manually, divide 100 by the number of questions (underlined words).This will give you the percentage value of each question. For instance, on a quiz with 12 questions, each would be worth 8.33 percentage points. Subtract that number for each wrong answer. The result is the quiz percentage score. As with computer scoring, divide the percentage score by 3.33 and round to the nearest number. This is the point grade for the quiz. Enter the number of points on the appropriate scoring sheet in chapter five.

Chapter Scores

Your student's chapter scores, given in weeks 14-26, will be based on a series of five rubrics worth 20 points each. Every week you'll need to read your student's chapter and assign a number between 1 and 20. Again, high numbers are better than low. The rubrics are consistent from week to week except for the final week, 26, which focuses on revision.

Create emotion: Regardless of anything else the chapter does or doesn't do, is it good at creating emotion? Does it make you *feel* anything when you read it? Or does it produce boredom, the lack of emotion? Reward emotion with a high score.

Compelling conflict: Is the chapter based on a tangible clash of wills? Is it either a disaster or a dilemma? If not, deduct points.

Value change: Is the chapter necessary? Does something change over the course of the chapter, or do things remain essentially the same? Good chapters show how something important to a chapter (a value) changes.

26

Weak chapters show things happening that don't have a specific bearing on the plot.

Incorporate story elements: Does the chapter incorporate the elements your student outlined in the first semester (the novel outline)? Does it use the answers in the Map, and if not, does it essentially do what *The Map* intended for this particular chapter?

Precise, unexpected details: Does the chapter create a movie in your mind as you read it? Does it rely on sensual imagery, or is it filled with adverbs and redundant adjectives? Deduct points if the chapter is conceptual in nature or filled with passive sentence constructions (an abundance of "was" sentences.)

The rubrics for week 26 are based on your student's revision of the entire novel, and should be self-explanatory: *spelling, punctuation, formatting*, and *adverbs/adjectives*.

Enter a number for each rubric on the appropriate score sheet in chapter five, then total the rubrics to determine each chapter's score.

Scoring Overview

Semester 1 (Weeks 1-13)

Daily Lesson
Complete	10 points
Appropriate	10 points
Well Though Out	10 points

	30 points
x 3 lessons / week	90 points

Weekly Quiz   30 points

                                                        120 points
                                                        x 13 weeks

Semester 1   = **1,560** points

Semester 2 (Weeks 14-26)

Weekly Chapter
Rubric 1	20 points
Rubric 2	20 points
Rubric 3	20 points
Rubric 4	20 points
Rubric 5	20 points

                                                        100 points

Weekly Quiz   30 points

                                                        130 points
                                                        x 13 weeks

Semester 2   = **1,690** points

4

Weekly Quizzes

The weekly quizzes printed in this chapter are also included on the Resource Disk as part of a software program. You can give the weekly quizzes manually, or let a computer do it for you.

To have your computer give a quiz, insert the Resource Disk and open the OYAN access screen in your browser. Double-click on the appropriate quiz for any given week and the quiz program will launch automatically. After your student answers the last question, the program will calculate a final score. Divide this by 3.33 and round to the nearest whole number. Enter this number on the score sheet in chapter five.

All 26 quizzes (complete with answers) are included on the following pages in case you don't have a computer or prefer to give each quiz verbally.

I should mention that I consider these quizzes to be of only minor importance, and have weighted their impact on the final grade accordingly.

This curriculum is more about application of storytelling technique than memorization. Therefore each weekly quiz is worth about the same amount of points as one daily lesson.

When giving the quizzes verbally, the underlined words should be read as blanks (i.e., " Your novel should be written in blank person point of view.")

QUIZ #1
Lessons 1 - 3

The three plot types we discussed briefly are: <u>Boy</u> Meets Girl, The <u>Man Who Learned</u> Better, and The <u>Heroic</u> Quest.

(T/F) Third person point of view is rare in fiction. (False)

(T/F) Your Hero can be any age. (False)

Your novel should be written in <u>first</u> person point of view.

A synopsis is divided into two parts, a <u>situation</u> and a <u>question</u>.

The first part of a synopsis consists of context, a Hero, and a Story <u>Goal</u>.

The second part of a synopsis consists of a villain, a price paid, and a <u>theme</u>.

Context means the way things <u>are</u>.

(T/F) The basic plot of every possible story has already been written in some form. (True)

QUIZ #2
Lessons 4 - 5

Name the five elements of story:
1. <u>Someone to Care About</u>
2. <u>Something to Want</u>
3. <u>Something to Dread</u>
4. <u>Something to Suffer</u>
5. <u>Something to Learn</u>

Something to Want is also called a <u>story goal</u>.

Character traits can be divided into the internal and the <u>external</u>.

Name three externals discussed in lesson 5:
1. <u>Undeserved Misfortune</u>
2. <u>Power with Humility</u>
3. <u>Weakness</u>

Characters, like people, are best defined by the <u>choices</u> they make.

All stories are interpreted through <u>moral</u> filters.

Name the three internals (other than choice) discussed in lesson 6:
1. <u>Morality</u>
2. <u>Desire</u>
3. <u>Will</u>

31

QUIZ #3
Lessons 7-9

The <u>Story</u> <u>Goal</u> is the driving force of your story.

(T/F) A Hero's inner motivation and outer motivation are always the same thing. (False)

Raising the stakes means giving your Hero more to <u>lose</u>.

Your Hero should represent a <u>positive</u> Ideal.

We tend to care about people we <u>know</u>.

(T/F) It is important for your reader to understand what the story goal is. (True)

The best story goals can be represented in a <u>single</u> <u>photographable</u> <u>act</u>.

(T/F) Another way of finding the story goal is to ask, "How will the audience know when the story is over?" (True)

QUIZ #4
Lessons 10 - 12

You create <u>suspense</u> by warning your audience that something bad is about to happen, and then <u>postponing</u> it.

Three ways of warning the audience about something bad about to happen to the Hero are:
1. Make it happen to <u>someone</u> else.
2. Create a <u>symbol</u> of dread.
3. Make your Hero <u>afraid</u> of something.

Dread is a combination of <u>curiosity</u>, expectation and fear.

<u>Conflict</u> is found where Something to Want meets Something to Dread.

The obstacles in your Hero's way should become increasingly <u>difficult</u>, and flow naturally from the conflict. Done well, this will produce a <u>rising</u> conflict.

A specific hint about a Bad Thing Around the Corner may be called a <u>Dreadful</u> <u>Promise</u>.

You must <u>fulfill</u> every Dreadful Promise.

You fulfill dreadful promises by making the thing we dread <u>worse</u> than expected.

Your <u>Villain</u> embodies the conflict.

QUIZ #5
Lessons 13 - 15

(T/F) Something is worth the highest price someone is wiling to pay for it. (True)

The suffering your Hero endures determines the <u>value</u> of your Story Goal.

The two types of suffering in any novel are <u>physical</u> and <u>emotional</u>.

<u>Emotional</u> suffering is the most effective kind of suffering in a novel.

(T/F) The suffering your Hero endures should build to a climactic point near the end of the story. (True)

List four types of physical suffering:
1. <u>inconvenience</u>
2. <u>discomfort</u>
3. <u>pain</u>
4. <u>loss</u>

QUIZ #6
Lessons 16 - 18

A <u>theme</u> is a short phrase that makes a general statement about some larger truth.

A <u>premise</u> is a one-sentence description of the theme that will be expressed through you novel's characters and conflict.

(T/F) A premise should contain an implied conflict and ending. (True)

You <u>novel</u> should be built on a <u>premise</u>, which should be built on a <u>theme</u>.

An <u>Ideal</u> is a goal, model or trait that signifies some larger force or state of perfection.

Name the four kinds of Ideals that will be expressed through your characters:
1. <u>Positive</u>
2. <u>Contrary</u>
3. <u>Negative</u>
4. <u>Reversed</u> or <u>Ironic</u>.

<u>Meaning</u> is one thing pointing to something else.

<u>Meaning</u> is usually expressed through <u>character</u> change or <u>revelation</u>.

(T/F) Your Hero must change from negative to positive in order for the character change technique to work. (False)

QUIZ #7
Lessons 19 - 21

The five character types we've discussed are:
1. <u>Hero</u>
2. <u>Villain</u>
3. <u>Mentor</u>
4. <u>Ally</u>
5. <u>Love</u>

Which character is not recommended for your adventure novel? (Love)

(T/F) The main difference between your Hero and your Villain is morality. (True)

(T/F) Your villain should not have any weaknesses. (False)

In order for your <u>villain</u> to be believable, he should be <u>human</u>. You can make him seem human by helping your reader to <u>understand</u> him.

A synopsis consists of a <u>situation</u> and a <u>question</u>.

The situation is:
1. The way things are, also called the <u>context</u>.
2. Someone to Care About, the <u>Hero</u>.
3. Something to Want, the <u>Story</u> <u>Goal</u>.

The question is:
1. Something to Dread, the <u>villain</u>.
2. Something to suffer, the <u>price</u>.
3. Something to learn, the <u>theme</u>.

QUIZ #8
Lessons 22-24

(T/F) Conflict is essential to storytelling. (True)

Conflict exists on the level of the novel, the act, the <u>situation</u>, and the <u>moment</u>.

(T/F) Beginning writers often fail to create believable conflict in every scene, on every page. (True)

Scenic or <u>situational</u> conflicts are like sword fights. <u>Momentary</u> conflicts are like the individual thrusts and parries of the fight.

External conflicts are called <u>Disasters</u>.

Internal conflicts are <u>Dilemmas</u>.

(T/F) The majority of your chapters should be dilemmas. (False)

(T/F) Disaster means that something goes terribly and unexpectedly wrong. (True)

Disasters should be <u>emotionally</u> charged.

A <u>dilemma</u> is a <u>scenic</u> conflict built on the internal <u>pressure</u> a character feels when forced to make a <u>decision</u> between two terrible <u>possibilities</u>.

A person's character is only revealed under <u>pressure</u>.

(T/F) Dilemmas only follow disasters. (True)

(T/F) You should never immediately follow one dilemma with another. (True)

QUIZ #9
Lessons 25-27

Your novel should have how many acts? (Three)

(T/F) A scene is the smallest section of a story in which something of value to the story changes. (True)

(T/F) Whenever characters change locations, you should start a new scene. (False)

(T/F) Every scene has a climactic turning point that shows a change of values. (True)

All scenes turn either on action or <u>revelation</u>. Either a character does something or he learns something.

You story will be defined by <u>four</u> (how many) major scenes or chapters. These define the boundaries of the <u>three</u> (how many) acts.

The first defining scene or chapter is called the <u>inciting</u> incident.

List the three most common types of novel openings:
1. The new <u>arrival</u>.
2. <u>Trouble</u>.
3. Some kind of <u>fight</u>.

Quiz #10
Lessons 28-30

Chapter three falls at the end of the <u>first</u> act.

Chapter three is called embracing <u>destiny</u>.

(T/F) Both the reluctant and the eager hero choose to seek the story goal no matter what the cost. (True)

The Act 2 climax is also called the black <u>moment</u>.

The black moment chapter is usually a <u>disaster</u> followed by a <u>dilemma</u>.

The black moment establishes your credibility as a narrator by planting <u>doubt</u> about the outcome in the reader's mind.

(T/F) The black moment dramatizes the price your Hero must pay in order to achieve the story goal. (True)

The Act 3 climax is also called the <u>showdown</u>.

To make your novel climax work, you must fulfill the story goal in an <u>unexpected</u> way.

QUIZ #11
Lessons 31-33

(T/F) Great stories rarely follow an established pattern. (False)

Good stories follow patterns in <u>unpredictable</u> ways. Good stories are <u>meaningful</u>.

A <u>subplot</u> is a secondary story within the framework of your novel. It is a complete story that intertwines with your main one.

(T/F) A subplot ought to have some bearing on the main story line. (True)

Chapter two might also be called Promises, Prophecies and <u>Predicaments</u>.

Dramatists sometimes refer to a <u>gap</u> between the expected and the actual. The main objective of chapter two is to <u>widen</u> it.

Chapter four often shows the Hero entering a <u>new</u> <u>world</u>.

(T/F) The mentor is often revealed as the mentor in chapter four. (True)

QUIZ #12
Lessons 34-36

The middle cycle consists of a repeating pattern of
1. forming a short term <u>goal</u>.
2. <u>pursuing</u> it.
3. problem or <u>difficulty</u>.
4. <u>reacting</u> to the problem and repeating the cycle.

Chapter six often shows the Hero's <u>failure</u>.

(T/F) Failure shows your reader that the Hero may not achieve the story goal and thereby heightens suspense. (True)

Chapter six is an excellent place to raise the <u>stakes</u>. This means giving your hero more to <u>lose</u>.

Chapter seven is also called <u>lessons</u>.

(T/F) It is possible to learn more from failure than from success. (True)

QUIZ #13
Lessons 37-39

Chapter eight is called <u>Atonement</u> and <u>Achievement</u>.

The goal of every story is to create <u>emotion</u>.

To atone for something means to make <u>amends</u> for it.

Chapter ten may also be called the coming <u>storm</u>.

Chapter ten should increase story <u>tension</u> and force us into the chapter 11 showdown. This is accomplished through a <u>rising</u> action that produces <u>complications</u> but not <u>delays</u>.

The three techniques for increasing story tension in this chapter are
1. significant <u>action</u>.
2. <u>time</u> bombs (also known as ticking clocks.)
3. unavoidable action and <u>choice</u>.

Chapter 12 is also called the <u>denouement</u>. (careful of the spelling)

One approach to writing the last chapter involves what Joseph Campbell called "<u>crossing</u> the return threshold." Another is to simply resolve a <u>subplot</u>.

QUIZ #14
Lessons 40-42

Seat of pants to seat of <u>chair</u>.

Writers <u>translate</u> imagination into words. Readers <u>translate</u> words into imagination.

Rough drafts are <u>rough</u>.

The writing process means
1. clearly and accurately <u>imagining</u> the story events in your outline.
2. clearly and accurately <u>describing</u> what you imagine.

(T/F) Grammar and spelling are extremely important in your initial rough draft. (False)

You should only interrupt the flow of your imagination for one question: What's <u>likely</u> to go <u>wrong</u>?

(T/F) You have many story templates in your memory. (True)

(T/F) The story templates in your memory are trustworthy sources of story events. (False)

(T/F) You don't need to make any promises to your reader. (False)

Your goal is to create emotion in your <u>reader</u>, not your characters.

(T/F) Creating emotion does not mean showing emotion. (True)

A story without emotion is <u>boring</u>.

(T/F) Your job as a writer is to recreate reality in your reader's mind. (False)

QUIZ #15
Lessons 43-45

The three modes of fiction are <u>Summary</u>, <u>Detail</u> and <u>Dialog</u>.

(T/F) Good writers always show; they never tell. (False)

(T/F) Summary is used to convey facts and anything unemotional. (True)

Detail mode means <u>showing</u>. It means giving your reader <u>precise</u> details that recreate in her own mind the story you imagine.

(T/F) Too many details will kill emotion. (True)

(T/F) Not enough detail will kill emotion. (True)

(T/F) Specific, meaningful details create emotion. (True)

Summary mode communicates to your reader's mind through her <u>mind</u>. Detail mode communicates to her <u>heart</u> through her <u>senses</u>.

Actions first, then <u>reactions</u>.

Put the following in proper narrative order: <u>Feelings</u>, <u>Thoughts</u>, <u>Action</u>, <u>Speech</u>.
>   (Feelings, Thoughts, Action, Speech)

QUIZ #16
Lessons 46-48

(T/F) Dialog means only the words between quotation marks. (False)

he said, is an example of a dialog <u>tag</u>.

(T/F) It will make your novel better to use wild and funky verbs in your dialog tags instead of said and asked. (False)

(T/F) Most communication is done verbally. (False)

Writers convey the tone of a spoken conversation through the language of <u>gestures</u>.

Good dialog creates <u>emotion</u>, moves the <u>plot</u> forward and reveals <u>character</u>.

(T/F) Passive voice creates ambiguity. (True)

(T/F) Passive voice should be cut ruthlessly from your novel. (True)

Passive voice reveals a weak <u>verb</u>, <u>tells</u> when it means to <u>show</u>, and always fails to convey <u>simultaneous</u> action.

Good description is a <u>verb</u>.

QUIZ #17
Lessons 49-51

Adverbs often indicate a weak <u>verb</u>.

Adjectives sometimes indicate an imprecise <u>noun</u>.

(T/F) It's okay to write as though inanimate objects have a mind of their own. (False)

(T/F) When something gets in the way of clarity, it usually hinders the reader's imagining of story events. (True)

The goal of every story is to create <u>emotion</u>.

Only use adjectives that are necessary and <u>precise</u>. Dull, <u>redundant</u> adjectives indicate you aren't seeing your story clearly.

A symbol of <u>dread</u> reminds the reader of the <u>conflict</u>.

QUIZ #18
Lessons 52-54

A <u>flashback</u> is a <u>memory</u> recounted as though its events were happening in the present. It is not just a scene placed out of chronological <u>order</u>.

(T/F) A flashback should have some bearing on the story goal. (True)

(T/F) Flashbacks should be avoided when possible. (True)

(T/F) Using "I saw" and "I heard" is usually not a good idea in fiction. (True)

(T/F) Always focus the camera lens of your sentence on the most interesting thing. (True)

Raising the <u>stakes</u> means giving your character more to <u>lose</u>. It means increasing the cost of <u>failure</u>.

The two ways of raising stakes discussed in this curriculum are:
1. Making the <u>danger</u> bigger.
2. Giving us more to <u>lose</u> emotionally.

Ask yourself three questions:
1. Why should your reader <u>care</u>?
2. How could this get <u>worse</u>?
3. How can there be more to <u>lose</u>?

QUIZ #19
Lessons 55-57

(T/F) Your rough draft is the best place to correct grammar and spelling. (False)

Give yourself <u>permission</u> to write badly.

(T/F) A feeling of boredom you get when writing may indicate a lack of conflict in the story. (True)

The only question your internal editor should ask you when writing a rough draft is, "What's likely to go <u>wrong</u>?"

One way of jump-starting a slow middle section is to drop a <u>body</u> out of the ceiling.

Your characters must behave as if they had a free <u>will</u>. They must only act out of their own <u>desire</u>. They must never <u>do</u> anything just because you want them to.

Your subconscious mind is good at problem-<u>solving</u>, but not very good at <u>communicating</u>.

QUIZ #20
Lessons 58-60

(T/F) Setting should infuse every aspect of your story. (True)

(T/F) Your novel's setting should help create emotion. (True)

Techniques for creating setting:
1. Precise <u>details</u>.
2. Showing how a character's reaction to place <u>changes</u> over time.

Historical settings are created by:
1. Historic <u>details</u> we don't <u>expect</u>.
2. Characters that act like real <u>people</u>.

Character <u>masks</u> are a writer's way of dealing with one emotion through another.

(T/F) Real people often hide their deepest emotions. (True)

Superficial physical traits can be used as character <u>handles</u> to quickly and clearly <u>identify</u> a character.

QUIZ #21
Lessons 61-63

The unexpected should impact your novel in three areas, unexpected <u>humor</u>, unexpected <u>tragedy</u>, and unexpected <u>grace</u>. (Make sure you put these in the order they are discussed in the textbook.)

(T/F) All humor is unexpected or it doesn't work. (True)

(T/F) Bad luck is usually believable. (True)

(T/F) Unfortunate events should come in multiples. Not just one bad thing, but two or three. (True)

(T/F) Good luck is usually believable. (False)

(T/F) Grace (or good luck) should happen as a natural result of something that happened previously in the story. (True)

(T/F) The feeling produced by good luck will last a long time in the reader. (False)

<u>Good</u> luck can be made <u>believable</u> by disguising it as <u>bad</u> luck.

QUIZ #22
Lessons 64-66

A <u>cliche</u> is an overused expression or phrase that is completely devoid of originality.

Cliches hurt your writing by:
A. Telling your reader you aren't original
B. Making the story unclear
C. Spoiling the ending
D. A and B (correct)
E. B and C

As a general rule, you should <u>avoid</u> describing things conceptually. Instead, use the <u>senses</u> to describe what you see, hear feel, taste and touch in your imagination.

A <u>plot</u> cliche is a situation you've seen so often it isn't unexpected.

<u>Irony</u> can be defined as something that simultaneously conveys opposite things.

<u>Situational</u> irony is also called cosmic irony.

<u>Dramatic</u> irony is when the audience knows more than the characters.

Socratic irony means feigning <u>ignorance</u> in order to draw someone else to the truth.

A <u>cliffhanger</u> refers to any plot situation that leaves the hero (and the audience) in an extended state of suspense.

End each chapter with a strong implied <u>question</u>.

QUIZ #23
Lessons 67-69

Your <u>voice</u> is an expression of your personality.

A writer's <u>literary</u> voice is his personality expressed on paper.

(T/F) The voice of the narrator and the voice of the writer are identical. (False)

The two kinds of voice discussed in lesson 67 are <u>narratorial</u> voice and authorial voice.

(T/F) Utter honesty and transparency are appealing to readers. (True)

<u>Conflict</u> is the essence of story.

Double disasters draw their <u>power</u> from the large initial disaster. The <u>first</u> disaster is shocking in its <u>size</u> and scope. The <u>second</u> feels shocking—feels worse than it is—because of its <u>timing</u>.

QUIZ #24
Lessons 70-72

A hero's actions must be based on <u>principle</u>, on his positive Ideal.

(T/F) An unresolved clash of ideals is frustrating. (True)

(T/F) Without a clear moral stance, a story is not a story. (True)

A story without a clear moral stance will lack <u>resolution</u>.

A story <u>climax</u> should have a clear moment of <u>decision</u>.

Climaxes focus on the <u>question</u>, "Will the Hero <u>attain</u> the story goal?" This creates <u>tension</u> that must be released in the <u>climax</u>.

(T/F) A setup/payoff is a container for significance that uses Detail Mode to get across meaning to your audience. (True)

Deus ex Machima means "God from the <u>machine</u>."

Never let your characters out of a story dilemma without <u>acting</u>. Never let the pressure off except as a result of something your Hero <u>does</u>.

Quiz #25
Lessons 73-75

Denouements generally:
1. Reduce <u>tension</u>
2. Decrease <u>time</u> pressure
3. Center on a <u>dilemma</u>.

Denouements usually resolve by:
1. Resolving <u>subplots</u>
2. Bringing the Hero back to the <u>old</u> world.

<u>Reward</u> or punish your Hero based on the clash of Ideals and the standards of the moral code.

The best ending paragraphs capture the sense of <u>fulfillment</u> your reader feels as a result of the clash of <u>ideals</u> in the <u>showdown</u> and the resulting <u>reward</u> demonstrated in the <u>denouement</u>.

Begin the process of revising your novel by leaving it alone for at least three <u>weeks</u>.

QUIZ #26
Lessons 76-78

<u>Verbs</u> are the active words that move your story forward.

Your manuscript should use 12 point <u>courier</u> as a font.

(T/F) Using colorful paper will make your story stand out and ensure it is read by an editor. (False)

5

Score Sheets

Use the chapter score sheets on pages 58 through 71 to record your student's weekly grades. These scores will be used to determine the final grade at the end of the year.

Week 1

     Lesson 1   _____ points

     Lesson 2   _____ points

     Lesson 3   _____ points

     Quiz #1   _____ points

     Week 1 Total   [   ]

Week 2

     Lesson 4   _____ points

     Lesson 5   _____ points

     Lesson 6   _____ points

     Quiz #2   _____ points

     Week 2 Total   [   ]

SCORE SHEETS

Week 3

       Lesson 7   _____ points

       Lesson 8   _____ points

       Lesson 9   _____ points

       Quiz #3   _____ points

       Week 3 Total   [   ]

Week 4

       Lesson 10   _____ points

       Lesson 11   _____ points

       Lesson 12   _____ points

       Quiz #4   _____ points

       Week 4 Total   [   ]

Week 5

Lesson 13 _____ points

Lesson 14 _____ points

Lesson 15 _____ points

Quiz #5 _____ points

Week 5 Total

Week 6

Lesson 16 _____ points

Lesson 17 _____ points

Lesson 18 _____ points

Quiz #6 _____ points

Week 6 Total

Week 7

Lesson 19	_____ points
Lesson 20	_____ points
Lesson 21	_____ points
Quiz #7	_____ points
Week 7 Total	

Week 8

Lesson 22	_____ points
Lesson 23	_____ points
Lesson 24	_____ points
Quiz #8	_____ points
Week 8 Total	

Week 9

Lesson 25   _____ points

Lesson 26   _____ points

Lesson 27   _____ points

Quiz #9   _____ points

Week 9 Total

Week 10

Lesson 28   _____ points

Lesson 29   _____ points

Lesson 30   _____ points

Quiz #10   _____ points

Week 10 Total

Week 11

Lesson 31 _____ points

Lesson 32 _____ points

Lesson 33 _____ points

Quiz #11 _____ points

Week 11 Total ☐

Week 12

Lesson 34 _____ points

Lesson 35 _____ points

Lesson 36 _____ points

Quiz #12 _____ points

Week 12 Total ☐

Week 13

        Lesson 37   _____ points

        Lesson 38   _____ points

        Lesson 39   _____ points

        Quiz #13   _____ points

        Week 13 Total

Semester 1 totals

add all weekly totals for weeks 1-13:

SCORE SHEETS

Week 14

Create emotion?	_____	(20 points)
Compelling conflict?	_____	(20 points)
Value change?	_____	(20 points)
Incorporate story elements?	_____	(20 points)
Precise, unexpected details?	_____	(20 points)
Quiz #14	_____	(30 points)

Week 14 Total

Week 15

Create emotion?	_____	(20 points)
Compelling conflict?	_____	(20 points)
Value change?	_____	(20 points)
Incorporate story elements?	_____	(20 points)
Precise, unexpected details?	_____	(20 points)
Quiz #15	_____	(30 points)

Week 15 Total

Week 16

Create emotion?	_____	(20 points)
Compelling conflict?	_____	(20 points)
Value change?	_____	(20 points)
Incorporate story elements?	_____	(20 points)
Precise, unexpected details?	_____	(20 points)
Quiz #16	_____	(30 points)

Week 16 Total [   ]

Week 17

Create emotion?	_____	(20 points)
Compelling conflict?	_____	(20 points)
Value change?	_____	(20 points)
Incorporate story elements?	_____	(20 points)
Precise, unexpected details?	_____	(20 points)
Quiz #17	_____	(30 points)

Week 17 Total [   ]

SCORE SHEETS

Week 18

Create emotion?	_____	(20 points)
Compelling conflict?	_____	(20 points)
Value change?	_____	(20 points)
Incorporate story elements?	_____	(20 points)
Precise, unexpected details?	_____	(20 points)
Quiz #18	_____	(30 points)

Week 18 Total

Week 19

Create emotion?	_____	(20 points)
Compelling conflict?	_____	(20 points)
Value change?	_____	(20 points)
Incorporate story elements?	_____	(20 points)
Precise, unexpected details?	_____	(20 points)
Quiz #19	_____	(30 points)

Week 19 Total

Week 20

Create emotion?	_____	(20 points)
Compelling conflict?	_____	(20 points)
Value change?	_____	(20 points)
Incorporate story elements?	_____	(20 points)
Precise, unexpected details?	_____	(20 points)
Quiz #20	_____	(30 points)

Week 20 Total

Week 21

Create emotion?	_____	(20 points)
Compelling conflict?	_____	(20 points)
Value change?	_____	(20 points)
Incorporate story elements?	_____	(20 points)
Precise, unexpected details?	_____	(20 points)
Quiz #21	_____	(30 points)

Week 21 Total

Week 22

Create emotion? _____ (20 points)

Compelling conflict? _____ (20 points)

Value change? _____ (20 points)

Incorporate story
    elements? _____ (20 points)

Precise, unexpected
    details? _____ (20 points)

Quiz #22 _____ (30 points)

Week 22 Total

Week 23

Create emotion? _____ (20 points)

Compelling conflict? _____ (20 points)

Value change? _____ (20 points)

Incorporate story
    elements? _____ (20 points)

Precise, unexpected
    details? _____ (20 points)

Quiz #23 _____ (30 points)

Week 23 Total

Week 24

Create emotion?	_____ (20 points)
Compelling conflict?	_____ (20 points)
Value change?	_____ (20 points)
Incorporate story elements?	_____ (20 points)
Precise, unexpected details?	_____ (20 points)
Quiz #24	_____ (30 points)

Week 24 Total

Week 25

Create emotion?	_____ (20 points)
Compelling conflict?	_____ (20 points)
Value change?	_____ (20 points)
Incorporate story elements?	_____ (20 points)
Precise, unexpected details?	_____ (20 points)
Quiz #25	_____ (30 points)

Week 25 Total

Week 26

Spelling?	_____	(20 points)
Punctuation?	_____	(20 points)
Adverbs/adjectives?	_____	(20 points)
Formatting	_____	(20 points)
Emotion?	_____	(20 points)
Quiz #26	_____	(30 points)

Week 26 Total

Semester 2 totals

add all weekly totals for weeks 14-26:

6

The Final Grade

To determine your student's final class grade, add together all weekly totals from both semesters.

Final Grading Scale

3,250 points possible

92% 2,990 points = A
84% 2,730 points = B
76% 2,470 points = C
68% 2,210 points = D

ONE YEAR
ADVENTURE
NOVEL

For more information, go to:

www.OneYearNovel.com

LaVergne, TN USA
31 August 2009
156462LV00002B/1/P